Thirty

Simple Prayers for Firefighters and First Responders

Samuel Lee Schmidt

THIRTY SIMPLE PRAYERS FOR FIREFIGHTERS AND FIRST RESPONDERS

Samuel Lee Schmidt

www.samuelministry.org

ISBN-10: 1976436311
ISBN-13: 978-1976436314

To all those who tirelessly work to keep the rest of

us safe from harm. Thank you.

every night I pray for
you to always return
home to me. always
safe and unharmed.
you mean the world
to me and I'm so
proud of you. I will
always support, encourage,
and love you.

Stay safe
my love
-Wifey ♡

INTRODUCTION

The one avenue of Jesus' ministerial life his disciples were so enamored with, was his ministry of prayer. They did not approach Jesus and say, "Teach us how to preach." They did not approach Jesus and say, "Teach us how to teach." They did not approach Jesus and say, "Teach us how to heal." The disciples approached Jesus and said, "Teach us how to *pray.*"

Prayer is the most powerful weapon in the arsenal of Christian warfare. Unfortunately, instead of a first line of defense, it's often used as a last resort. Would you commit just thirty days to improving your prayer life?

Don't neglect the power of prayer.

Pray continuously,
Samuel

HOW TO USE THIS BOOK

These are simple prayers, meant to be used in simple ways. These prayers are not elaborate, nor are they long. These prayers are written as a form of devotion and encouragement. They are written specifically for those who serve in a first responder capacity.

The proper way to go through this book would be to read one prayer each day, for thirty days. After thirty days, consider reading the book again. After another thirty days have passed, consider reading the book once more. Ultimately, you should consider memorizing these prayers. Meditate on them and reflect on their purpose. If you read just one prayer, each day, you will have made a habit of prayer after thirty days.

At the end, a *prayer journal* has been included, giving you a dedicated place to meditate on your prayer concerns. Consider writing down prayer needs you have, and making a note *how* God answers the prayer. Use this as a way to develop your personal prayer ministry.

Make prayer an obligation, not an option. Be diligent in your prayer life and God will richly reward you.

1

Thank You, Father, that you have opened the door for me to serve my community as a first responder. Help me not to take this opportunity lightly. Instill in me an eternal desire to serve others by putting them before my needs and wants. Keep me safe this day.

Amen.

2

Thank You, Father, for giving me the opportunity to serve others. I ask that today You keep me from physical harm, while I protect those around me, and serve my local community.

Amen.

3

Thank You, Father, for giving me the opportunity to be

a leader in my community. Help me to serve those

around me, and help those who are in need. Teach me

to understand the importance of putting others before

myself, regardless of my selfishness.

Amen.

4

Thank You, Father, for life that you have given me. I ask that You direct my life to its purpose. I want to be used by You to help others in their time of need.

Amen.

5

Thank You, Father, for giving me the opportunity to live in such a wonderful country. I am grateful for the opportunities You have given me in this life to be a citizen who gives back to my community.

Amen.

6

Thank You, Father, for giving me all that I have. I

acknowledge I am nothing without You. Teach me

patience today, as I serve in a stress filled

environment, endeavoring to put others before myself.

Amen.

7

Thank You, Father, for offering forgiveness to all who would accept it. I pray You would teach me to give forgiveness to others who have not earned it, and who do not deserve it, just as You have shown forgiveness to me. Thank You, for Your forgiveness.

Amen.

8

Thank You, Father, for direction and hope for my future. You have given me a path to walk on, and I pray You would instill in my heart a desire to faithfully pursue all that You have for me.

Amen.

9

Thank You, Father, for all of those who serve in positions of authority in my community. I ask that You help me submit to those who are over me, encouraging me to be a good steward with my time and energy.

Amen.

10

Thank You, Father, for giving me an employment opportunity that allows me to serve other people. I ask that You instill in me a strong work ethic that is pleasing to my supervisors and employer.

Amen.

11

Thank You, Father, for Your perfect will in my life. I don't always understand why things happen the way that they do, but I submit to Your plan and purpose for my path. Direct and guide my steps so I may serve You faithfully with all my energy.

Amen

12

Thank You, Father, for the wonderful world You created. Your marvelous creation is a direct representation of what a marvelous Father You are. Teach me to be in awe of all you have brought about.

Amen.

13

Thank You, Father, for loving me, when I was unlovable. As I encounter many different individuals from many different walks of life today, help me to love those who do not appear to be lovable, just as You have loved them.

Amen.

14

Thank You, Father, for giving me the strength to move forward when life seems difficult and unfair. I am grateful for all You have done in my life, and I commit to serving You and others with this day.

Amen.

15

Thank You, Father, for those who live in my community. Inspire me to serve my community faithfully, as You would have me. Teach me to love those around me, even as You have loved me.

Amen.

Thank You, Father, for giving me another day of life.

Today I ask that You keep me safe, as I seek to serve

others who are in need. Protect my family and those

around me from all harm.

Amen.

17

Thank You, Father, for my fellow coworkers and laborers serving in various first responder capacities around me. I pray today You would keep them safe from harm, and direct them on paths of righteousness.

Amen.

18

Thank You, Father, for the people who surround me. I ask that You would create in me a desire to minister to those closest to me, and encourage me to encourage them and serve them with all that I am.

Amen.

19

Thank You, Father, for being a righteous judge. Life does not always seem fair, but I am trusting in Your great plan and purpose for humanity. Help me to not pass judgement on those who do not deserve it.

Amen.

20

Thank You, Father, for giving me clarity of mind. I ask today that You would help me to be sober-minded in all that I do, not reacting to others harshly, or in times of emotion, but calm and collected as needed.

Amen.

21

Thank You, Father, for giving me life yet again. Today

I pray that You would guard me, even as I seek to

guard others. Protect me as I desire to protect others.

Guide me as I desire to guide others.

Amen.

22

Thank You, Father, for wisdom which comes from heaven. I acknowledge I need Your wisdom every moment of my profession. Help me to be spiritually wise in all that I do, as I serve my community and those who are around me.

Amen.

23

Thank You, Father, for the home You have provided for me. I am encouraged and grateful for all You have brought about in my life. Thank You for Your continued mercy and grace upon me, even when I do not deserve it.

Amen.

Thank You, Father, for giving me strength for today. I ask now that You would strengthen my back for the labor of the day. Keep my strong and vigilant in my service to You and those around me.

Amen.

25

Thank You, Father, for those first responders who have given their life in service of others. I pray that I would not forget the major sacrifice so many have given in the service of their community. I ask that You keep my safe today in all my endeavors.

Amen.

26

Thank You, Father, for giving purity to those who seek it. Today I ask You would keep me pure from the impurities of life, guarding me against the temptations and schemes of the world. Keep my thoughts pure, and my mind focused on heavenly matters.

Amen.

27

Thank You, Father, for the gift of encouragement. You encourage me when I am weak. I ask that You would help me to encourage those around me today, ministering with my mouth to those in need.

Amen.

28

Thank You, Father, for those who serve alongside me in first responder roles. Today, I ask that You allow me to watch over my coworkers and fellow laborers, keeping them safe from harm. As others watch over me, help me to watch over them.

Amen.

29

Thank You, Father, for the enjoyment that comes from living a faithful life. Today I seek to be faithful to those in need, being a person of faithfulness and fairness. Help me to do my work with all diligence and faithfulness.

Amen.

Thank you, Father, for the place You have called me to

serve. As I protect and serve those around me, help me

to never forget the protection You have given over me

in my line of duty. You have kept me safe and secure,

and for that I am ever grateful.

Amen.

PRAYER GUIDE

_____

_____

_____

_____

_____

_____

_____

_____

_____

_____

_____

_____

For more information, visit www.samuelministry.org

For a free E-Book on prayer, visit
http://www.samuelministry.org/free-book/

Resources from the Samuel Ministry include:
- Spiritual discernment and assessment
- Preaching
- Teaching
- Sunday School
- Youth Ministry Labs
- And much more…

The Samuel Ministry is proud to offer the following
publications:

- *Preaching Pointers from the Book of Joel*
- *Thirty Simple Sermon Outlines for Any Occasion*
- *101 Simple Sermon Outlines for Any Occasion: Old Testament Edition*
- *Thirty Simple Prayers For Times of Devotion*
- *Thirty Simple Prayers For Police Officers and Law Enforcement*
- *Walking with Luther: A 30 Day Devotional in Honor of History's Greatest Reformer*
- *Joyfully Justified Because of Jesus*

Contact us for free ministry and discipleship resources.

Made in the USA
Middletown, DE
23 November 2018